C000039387

the Total Superiority *of the* NEW COVENANT

Companion Booklet to the video course by

DEAN BRIGGS

The Total Superiority of the New Covenant

to Apostolic Foundations Course 1

DEAN BRIGGS

CHAMPION PRESS

THE TOTAL SUPERIORITY OF THE NEW COVENANT:
COMPANION BOOKLET
© 2019 by Dean Briggs
Published by Champion Press
Kansas City, Missouri, USA

Unless otherwise indicated, all Scripture quotations are from
The ESV® Bible (The Holy Bible, English Standard
Version®), copyright © 2001 by Crossway, a publishing
ministry of Good News Publishers. Used by permission. All
rights reserved. Scripture quotations noted KJV are from the
KING JAMES VERSION of the Holy Bible.

Library of Congress Cataloging Publication Data
Briggs, Dean, 1968–
The Total Superiority of the New Covenant by Dean Briggs
ISBN: 9798663010795 (trade paper)

Other Books by Dean

NON-FICTION

- *Ekklesia Rising*
- *The Coming Great Blood Communion Revival*
- *Consumed: 40 Days of Fasting & Rebirth*
- *The Jesus Fast* (co-authored with Lou Engle)
- *Longhairs Rising*
- *Brave Quest: A Boy's Journey to Manhood*
- *Partakers of the Divine* (Parts 1-2)
- *Apostolic Foundation Series (Courses 1-5)*

FICTION (under D. Barkley Briggs)

- *The Legends of Karac Tor* (5 vol)
- *The Withering Tree*
- *The God Spot*
- *The Most Important Little Boy in the World*

WHAT OTHERS ARE SAYING
AFTER TAKING COURSE 1

"I have been a Christian for almost 40 years and never really understood these truths. I thought, what hope is there for me? How can I overcome these weaknesses? Now I see the truth and I can lay down my striving and accept His lavish grace."
— *H. Craig*

"This course has opened my eyes to the reality of who God is, and what living in the New Covenant really means. So much weight has been lifted. So much fresh revelation."
— *N. Comeau*

"I felt infused with understanding and revelation. It gives me language for what God has been doing inside of me."
— *C. Fowler*

"What an eye opener! Totally challenged to go deeper and have my mind renewed, understanding what Jesus did at the Cross."
— *L. Milton*

"I am full after what I've learned, yet hungry for more. This will be a game changer for me."
— *A. Christensen*

"Amazing teaching! We need more of this!"
— *D. Morais*

"Answers so many questions and released my mindset on the Old/New Covenant. I feel like I just got saved! So undone to know how much God loves us."
— *C. Gainforth*

"My fundamental belief about the grace of God has been forever changed."
— *K. Awuah*

"This course was an answer to prayer, and the beginning of deeper revelation, opening doors to where the riches of His glory in the saints are revealed. It's like a new dimension!"
— *P. Melanson*

"It wasn't information, it was revelation. I was confronted, not just presented, with truths that gave the Holy Spirit access to begin delivering me from many ungodly beliefs I have accumulated over the years."
— *T. Russell-Chipp*

"The truth shall set you free. Dean pointed us so beautifully to the Truth of the Person of Jesus. I am becoming enamored by Jesus and can't wait for more."
— *L. N.*

"Treasures unfolded to me. Thank you!"
— *G. Rathod*

"I am beginning to understand the practicalities of New Covenant living."
— *D. Mackenzie*

INTRODUCTION
Hebrews Chapter 8

6 "But as it is, **Christ has obtained a ministry that is as much more excellent than the old as the covenant he mediates is better, since it is enacted on better promises.**

7 **For if that first covenant had been faultless, there would have been no occasion to look for a second.**

8 For he finds fault with them when he says:
   "**Behold, the days are coming, declares the Lord, when I will establish a new covenant** with the house of Israel and with the house of Judah,

9 **not like the covenant that I made with their fathers** on the day when I took them by the hand to bring them out of the land of Egypt. For they did not continue in my covenant, and so I showed no concern for them, declares the Lord.

10 For this is the covenant that I will make with the house of Israel after those days, declares the Lord:
    I will put my laws into their minds,
    and write them on their hearts,
    and I will be their God, and they shall be my people.

11 And they shall not teach, each one his neighbor
    and each one his brother, saying, 'Know the Lord,'
    for **they shall all know me,**
    from the least of them to the greatest.

12 **For I will be merciful toward their iniquities,**
    and I will remember their sins no more."

The Total Superiority of the New Covenant

WHAT ARE COVENANTS
AND WHY DO THEY MATTER?

Houston, we have a problem—a big one. The Body of Christ has theoretically set its hope upon a salvation far greater than we truly understand, live for, or practically believe in. We have a gospel of salvation, a gospel of justice, even a gospel of *Churchianity*, but the ancient, apostolic gospel — "the faith that was once for all delivered to the saints" (Jude 1:3) — has become quite muddled, mixed, and diluted over centuries of religious thought.

Scholar Robert Mounce says, "The NT speaks of the gospel in a way that describes its benefits: it is 'the gospel of God's grace' (Acts 20:24), 'the gospel of salvation' (Eph. 1:13), 'the gospel of peace' 6:19), and the gospel that holds out hope (Col. 1:23). The gospel is worth dying for (Mark. 8:35; 10:29; Acts 20:24-25)."

Obviously, the gospel holds great and diverse riches, but do you know them beyond the promise of escape from hell and entrance into heaven? Do you know them beyond "spiritual gifts?" Do you know them beyond transforming the Seven Mountains? When angels first announced the arrival of the

Messiah, they said His coming would bring great joy to the human soul. Why?

"Good news of great joy!" the heavenly choir sang in the cold, starlit night above the hills of Bethlehem. "Peace on earth, goodwill (favor) toward men."

That word in Greek, *evangelion* ("good news!" from which we derive our English word, 'gospel') was not invented by Matthew, Mark, Luke or John. It actually enjoyed wide usage in the ancient Roman world and referred to the announcement of "glad tidings" regarding an emperor's birthday, rise to power, or decree that heralded the fulfillment of hopes for peace and well-being across the world. Mark redefines this concept of "glad tidings" by introducing his gospel with the phrase, "the beginning of the good news of Jesus Christ," (Mark 1:3) implying that it is really the birth and subsequent actions of Jesus that will change the face of the world in a cosmic way that no earthly king could ever do.

But proper perception and reception of the gospel of truth requires proper definition. This is what it means to evangelize: not simply to boldly "witness" to others or "share Jesus" so people can get forgiven or "saved." A huge altar call may represent genuine salvation but very little evangelism if it lacks faith to see Jesus and His mission more clearly and thereby produce mature disciples.

I'm talking about the "depth of the riches and wisdom and knowledge of God" (Rom. 11:33) that goes far beyond our initial experience of salvation. If they contemplate such things at all, most "believers" feel only a vague, fuzzy sense of longing for such things. They wonder if, in fact, there is more to their walk with God than merely the grunt work of life. Apostolic preaching is dedicated to bringing clarity and revelation to the Body of Christ so that we can fully believe all that we are intended to *perceive* and therefore *receive*. In fact, Paul described his job in 2 Corinthians 4:1 as a "steward of the mysteries of Christ" and to "preach the unsearchable mysteries of His grace" (Eph. 3:8).

The measure by which you should judge the teachings covered in both this introductory booklet and the full course include: *1) Are they biblical? 2) Does the Spirit bear witness? 3) Do they glorify Christ and increase your desire to know Him?*

To understand the fullness of God's plan means we must cover a scope of redemption far greater than John 3:16. We need to start at the beginning and get a clear grasp of who God is, how He thinks and operates, how He has intervened in history, and how He designed man to function and relate to Him in the world. To do this properly, we need a clear understanding of God's covenantal nature. How does God relate to man? Since creation itself, God's manner of interaction with humanity — the principles that govern these interactions — have been defined by a series of *covenants*. In general terms, a covenant is like a compact or contract, though far more serious, containing a specific series of requirements and pledges where God informs people about how He wants them to behave but also makes certain promises that will be enacted in various circumstances. Thus, a reasonable working definition of covenant is: *an unchangeable, divinely imposed, legal agreement between God and man that stipulates the conditions of their relationship.*

In other words, covenant helps us make sense of what we read in Scripture. Certain things happen for a reason! In modern times, we might read headlines of major events in the world, perhaps rumors of a war or one business suing another. These events might seem surprising, random or arbitrary, yet behind the scenes, lawyers, politicians, diplomats and generals are likely discussing various historic treaties and agreements previously enacted containing specific terms that are now being violated in some fashion. In other words, there is a story *behind* the story, but you can't actually make sense of the headlines unless you know about those agreements. The covenants of Scripture are similar. They are an invisible, driving force behind biblical narratives spanning thousands of years. Much of the logic and rationale of divine behavior is explained by covenant because God generally intervenes in history in a manner that is inaugurated and/or sustained by defined terms contained in covenantal language.

Biblically, covenants fall into two categories: covenants of performance or covenants grace. Similarly, our responsibility to these two types of covenants is either to obey the code, law, or terms of the Covenants of Performance, where Covenants of Grace are received by faith. The coming of Jesus and His finished work on the Cross contains, brings to maturity, and fully encompasses every other covenant. He is the *final* word, the *final* message, the *final* covenant by which all other lesser expressions must be understood.

Unfortunately, the word "covenant" has been used so frequently and with such elementary understanding that we end up smearing these words together in our minds as if all covenants are the same. Our Bibles are divided into the old covenant (Old Testament) and new covenant (New Testament), so it's all the same, right? Right? Actually, depending on how you count them, Scripture records seven covenants (though some only count five):

1. Creation (by inference and language)
2. Adamic
3. Noahic
4. Abrahamic
5. Mosaic (Old)
6. Davidic
7. Christ (New)

Do all seven essentially serve the same purpose? Do they have the same value and require the same allegiance? Do they cover the same span of time? For that matter, what is a covenant even for? Does it have any bearing on our life now?

The answers to these questions matter far more than you might realize. Chances are, the way you think (or don't think) about these crucial, foundational, spiritual dynamics dramatically affects your walk with God. Before we wade too much further into deeper waters, let's get our vocabulary

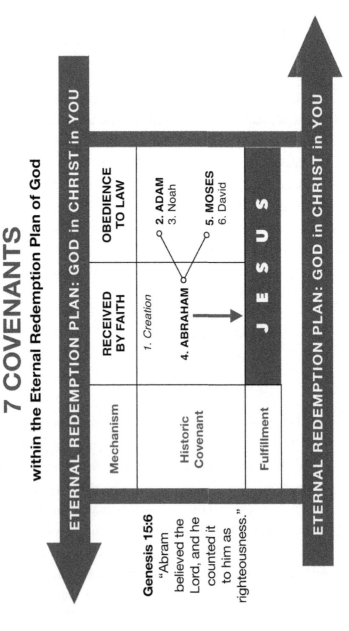

7 COVENANTS

within the Eternal Redemption Plan of God

ETERNAL REDEMPTION PLAN: GOD in CHRIST in YOU

Mechanism	RECEIVED BY FAITH	OBEDIENCE TO LAW	
Historic Covenant	*1. Creation* 4. ABRAHAM	**2. ADAM** 3. Noah **5. MOSES** 6. David	**J E S U S**
Fulfillment			

Genesis 15:6
"Abram believed the Lord, and he counted it to him as righteousness."

ETERNAL REDEMPTION PLAN: GOD in CHRIST in YOU

The Total Superiority of the New Covenant

straight. I'll tease out some differences, but in general, for the purpose of this course and booklet, the two major covenants are called Old and New, and are generally understood as the Covenant of Law given to Moses at Mount Sinai, followed by the Covenant of Grace enacted by Jesus in His death and resurrection.

The premise of *The Total Superiority of the New Covenant* is simple: The New Covenant is dramatically and intentionally superior to the Old in every way. It is fundamental to God's eternal plan, revealed in Christ, but woefully underdeveloped in modern discipleship. However, we cannot get where we need to go unless we reclaim the full power of the New Covenant to bring about the fullness of New Creation life.

WHAT'S SO GOOD ABOUT THE GOOD NEWS?

Remember, gospel simply means "good news"...so what's so good about it? Did Jesus come to create a "world religion" or simply make people behave better? Is the gospel a system of moralism?

Getting people saved and delivered from hell is *good*, but is that the good news? Attempting to eradicate abortion, sex trafficking, and poverty are all good things but are they the gospel? Discipling and equipping people to walk in their calling is awesome. Is that the good news?

Acceptance of different gospels has led to at least a fivefold crisis in the Church.

1. Where we should have clarity of the story, we have confusion.
2. Where we should have bold proclamation, we lack confidence.
3. Where we should be a leavening influence, we retreat from society or become/mirror it.
4. Where we should demonstrate love, we judge and condemn ourselves & others.

The Total Superiority of the New Covenant

5. Where we should experience personal power liberation and transformation, we remain in bondage, guilt, and weakness.

Imagine going bowling with some friends. When you get there, they immediately raise the kiddie lane bumpers. Do you protest? If so, why? Is the point to learn to bowl and get a strike, or is the point to avoid the gutters? If you bowl a perfect 300 using the kiddie bumpers, does that mean you are a great bowler?

Clearly, no. There are lesser goals and there are ultimate goals. The gospel has an ultimate goal, but we have increasingly defined it by a series of lesser goals. The transforming, liberating mystery of the gospel is far more than behavior conformity or even your eternal residence.

To demonstrate this, let me give you a great sounding theological statement: "The gospel is the news that "Jesus Christ, the Righteous One, died for our sins and rose again, eternally triumphant over all his enemies, so that there is now no condemnation for those who believe, but only everlasting joy. *That's* the gospel."

I like it! It's beautiful and glorious...but faulty, since the gospel is not a system describing how people get saved. Here's a better one: "The gospel is the proclamation of a perfect King and His perfect kingdom invading our broken world to redeem and restore humanity and elevate us to fellowship with Him forever."

That's also good, but as a matter of degrees, we're still off course. The trouble lies in this: as a matter of time and distance, veering even a little bit off course leads to a *lot* off course. Let me give you an example: You take off in an airplane intending to circumnavigate the globe only once. Departing from the equator, you are one degree off a true, flat, east-west latitude. But hey, it's only one degree! Oops. By the time you return to your original longitude, *you will be 400 miles off course.*

Degrees matter.

Now imagine if we rank degrees by centuries and millennia. How much of the apostolic gospel has been lost? Since the time of Martin Luther in the 1500s, we have been in a Reformation cycle, which is essentially a series of corrective measures for the sake of restoring what had previously been lost or neglected, but Peter, in the Book of Acts, said that Jesus would remain in heaven "until the restoration of all the things" (Acts 3:21 NKJV).

Not only is the gospel being restored, but the gospel itself is a restoration story. Redemptive history is a play in three acts.

- **ACT 1: "The Collapse"** — The curtain barely rises before Original Sin (unbelief, leading to rebellion) has spoiled the glorious Original Design of God, leaving humanity bereft of their full stature and status as the image of God. God's "Dominion Mandate" to humanity was forfeited for a poisonous bite of fruit. Ruler became slave, son became orphan, a blessed creation became cursed, and death now reigns. In the midst of an ancient cosmic war that predates human history, creation itself collapses. Everything collapses.

- **ACT 2: "The Rescue"** — Yet as powerful as <u>Original Sin</u> seemed in its potency to ruin the glorious purpose of God, it is about to be matched and totally overwhelmed by <u>Original Love</u>. God is faithful and unchanging. He is *with* us, *for* us, and therefore became *as* us, so that He could dwell *in* us. This story will unfold for countless centuries but will not fully manifest until Christ is revealed and announces the inauguration of His kingdom on earth. This kingdom turns weakness into power, power into weakness, and challenges the kingdom of darkness in every way, every place, in every person.

- **ACT 3: "The Restoration"** — The <u>Original Plan</u> was always about restoration, about elevating a fallen thing to an even more noble stature than it formerly enjoyed. It is in this sense that "creation was subjected to futility" (Rom. 8:20). At a level of mystery beyond human fathoming, veering off course was part of the sovereign design. Why? So that for eternity we would be guarded by humility upon our full restoration to <u>Original Design</u>. Thus, there is plus at the end. It is the <u>Original Plan+</u>. This is because, biblically, to restore something is to bring it to a stature better than its original state. We are heading to a future that is *better* than Eden, and we are meant to live the great abundance of that promise...*now.*

Since the New Covenant is dramatically and unequivocally better than the Old Covenant, it follows that the New Creation is dramatically and unequivocally better than the Old Creation. We are meant to live a totally new kind of life, but unless we understand the terms and dynamics by which the New Covenant produces New Creation Life, we can technically be recipients of grace, truly saved and born again, but living under the inferior dictates of an old system that God Himself intended to relegate to obsolescence.

Let me say it more succinctly: You can be a New Covenant believer but still live under slavery as an Old Covenant Christian. Sadly, hundreds of millions of Christians do this every day and have lived this way for generations. How can you know if you are one of them? There are tell-tale signs. Are you...

- Spiritually and emotionally worn out?
- Exhausted with striving?
- Constantly aware of your sin?
- Unable to overcome habitual sin?
- Constantly measuring your failures and judging yourself?

- Morally succeeding in a manner that only makes you proud and judgmental of others?
- Lacking vitality, brightness and a sense of real connection to God?
- Generally detached from the experience of the abundant life Jesus described and embodied?
- Trapped in almost schizophrenic swings between highs and lows of faith and doubt?
- Constantly doubtful of the fundamental goodness of God's nature and intentions?

I could go on and on, but you get the point. If this list describes you, chances are you unknowingly related to God from an Old Covenant heart. This booklet and, more completely, the full 58-session course (7-15 min each) have been specifically designed to help 1) reorient your focus, 2) repair faulty foundations in your core belief system, 3) realign your central paradigm, and 4) liberate and inspire faith by the power of anointed revelation, thereby, 5) setting you on a path to life as God designed, filled with mystery, beauty, connection, communion, grace, faith, blessings, and miracles.

The late Chinese writer and teacher, Watchman Nee, called this "The Normal Christian Life."

Thus, Course One cannot begin arbitrarily here or there. It *must* begin with covenantal realities, for the covenantal language of scripture forms the substructures of faith. Certainly, an entire series could be devoted to the nature of God, which is the most *eternal* foundation of all, but insofar as human interaction with God is concerned, covenant is and must be the beginning of the apostolic gospel. Covenant is the foundation everything else must be built upon. By beginning here, and exploring this pivotal aspect of our relationship to God, the happy by-product is that we *can* and *will* come to understand His eternal nature, also.

THE HEART OF
OUR HEART PROBLEM

"Return, O faithless sons;

I will heal your faithlessness" (Jer. 3:22a)

Question: How do you heal faithlessness? How do you objectively reverse or transform a fundamentally emotional/spiritual construct? Since a leopard cannot change its spots (Jer. 13:23), this is the great dilemma of a God committed to restoring His fallen creation while not yielding central values such as freewill and voluntary love. Since God is fundamentally good, He longs to bless and provide for us as sons — "How I would set you among my sons...and I thought you would call me, My Father" (Jer. 3:19) — so in our wayward, broken exile, He committed Himself to restoring nothing less than full relationship to Himself as our Father. This is a promise of the new and better covenant to come, because it was precisely Israel's disobedience (read: their unfaithfulness) to the terms of the old covenant that predicated their orphaned condition. But wait, the old covenant had so much awe and wonder! The radiant ark of the covenant, overshadowed by cherubim; the shekinah glory; the thundering mountain of God; the pillar of fire. But Jeremiah shocks us. In our full adoption as sons, God is going to do something surprising.

> **"In those days, declares the Lord, they shall no more say, 'The ark of the covenant of the Lord.' It shall not come to mind or be remembered or missed; it shall not be made again" (vs. 16).**

The New Covenant promises that there would no longer be an external ark of the covenant, not a golden box but a converted soul and an awakened spirit. So much of our discipleship wastes time trying to manipulate people into faithfulness with wrong motivations of dutiful compliance, sentimental loyalty, moral coercion, and guilt. Basically, try harder to prove your love! *This is inherently contradictory, even futile, when the disease is faithlessness.*

External pressure and conformity to a code of behavior will never heal the profoundly internal problem of a faithless heart. Thus, in the brilliant plan of God, He is going to relocate the ark of His Presence. But remember, the ark was called the "Ark of the Covenant." Covenant moves *inside.* The Old Covenant — external, written on stone — enlarges through Christ until all things become new. In this scenario, the burden of faithfulness becomes His, not ours. The task of obedient sonship becomes His, not ours. The problem of guilt becomes His, not ours. And in response, the privilege and blessings of Christ become ours, because of Him! You don't prove faithful to God with more effort, you simply fall into the mercy and grace of His perfect devotion and are thereby vindicated, made righteous, and filled with His faithful, devoted, *Holy* Spirit. The ark is no longer without, but within, because Christ is within. And this is our (only) hope: "Christ in you, the hope of glory" (Col. 1:27).

Listen, God doesn't heal faithlessness, in the sense of propping up and repairing a broken thing. No, actually, He judges it. He crucified our faithlessness in the body of His faithful Son, who then rose and ascended, and now takes residence within by the indwelling power of His Holy Spirit, purging our orphan status and invites us to think and act like royal heirs. The New Covenant takes that stony, selfish, wounded, fearful heart of unbelief and rebellion and makes it a living heart of flesh.

CONDEMNATION
OR SURPASSING GLORY

"For if there was glory in the *ministry of condemnation,*
the *ministry of righteousness must far exceed it in glory.*
Indeed, in this case, what once had glory has come to
have no glory at all, because of *the glory that surpasses
it*" (2 Cor. 3:9-10).

I n this verse, the Apostle Paul establishes many points of contrast between Law and Grace. I encourage you to study all of chapter 3 for yourself. It's so rich and represents one of Paul's clearest, most direct contrasts between the works of Moses and Christ. The ministry of condemnation clearly points to the law of Moses and the covenant God made at Sinai, while the ministry of righteousness is the work of the Spirit through the new and better Covenant of Grace.

Here's how it shakes down. In the chart below, left to right represents the progression (literally, progress! — not just chronology of time) of Old Covenant to New Covenant.

Old Covenant	—>	New Covenant
Ministry of condemnation	—>	Ministry of righteousness
Letter	—>	Spirit
Veiled	—>	Unveiled
Bondage	—>	Freedom
Written on stone	—>	Written on flesh

In dealing with our faithless hearts, the people of God have to finally settle and submit to what God has known all along: Law will only prove your unfaithfulness. That's the point of it! Law does not create unfaithfulness, it demonstrates it. You *are* unfaithful. You were born that way, and the Law brings you to full recognition of your guilt. The Law of Moses was meant to restrain our innate inclination toward sin, yet in the act of doing so, it further provokes it and, thereby, proves its stubborn, unyielding strength. This is the story of Romans 7. You were born that way because you were born into Adam. If you want to be born again, you must be born into Christ. Once you are in Christ, there is no reason to go back to the a temporary restraint system that is inferior to the interior work of Christ. The Law itself recognized and prophesied this reality when it proclaimed the need for a deep, inner work that fundamentally surpassed the external nature of the code in stone.

> **"And the Lord your God will circumcise your heart
> and the heart of your offspring, so that you will**

**love the Lord your God with all your heart and
with all your soul, that you may live" (Deut. 30:6).**

Do you see? The first explicit whisper of the New
Covenant extends all the way back to the booming oaths of the
ministry of condemnation. Clearly, God was saying, "This shall
not stand forever."

So when Paul says we are now "partakers of the promise in
Christ Jesus through the gospel" (Eph. 3:6), we must ask: which
promise? Galatians 3:29 makes clear that the promise is the one
made to Abraham, not Moses, otherwise it would not be a
promise, but a command. This is a covenant of grace, not law.
(By the way, such language could not have been more shocking
to the sensibilities of both Jew and Gentile. Specifically, Paul is
saying that outcast Gentiles are now "heirs together with Israel"
. . . as if they *had always been Abraham's blood kin.*

The dramatic, almost incomprehensible fact is that
salvation is not nearly so small as a Sinner's Prayer
accompanied by spiritual regeneration. Rather, it is literally
God extending to you the full covenant He made with
Abraham, yet enlarging it even more so that your inheritance is
actually everything Christ is, was, offers, and possesses.
Salvation is not merely a decision or a prayer; it is cutting
covenant with God. Far more importantly: *He cuts covenant
with you!*

What does "cutting" covenant mean? The ancient practice
of "cutting covenant" was a sober process intended to join two

parties together in a binding life-agreement. Typically, one of greater strength (a king or chieftain) would cut covenant with one of lesser strength. The greater would provided certain benefits to the weaker party, while the weaker of the two would pledge their loyalty and services to the greater. To ratify the agreement, the two parties would conduct a ritual with sacrificial animals, typically in the presence of other witnesses, wherein the animals would literally be cut in half. The two halves would then be spread apart, forming a trough of freshly spilled blood in the middle. The two parties would then recite the terms of their agreement and walk together through the bloody middle, staining the hems of their long robes. They were basically saying to each other, "Let the same sort of judgement and terror fall upon me as befell these animals, even at the risk of my own life, if I do not keep my word and pledge to you." Thus, to "cut covenant" goes far beyond our modern notions of treaties and contracts.

Now let me say it again. In the New Covenant, on the cross, *God cut covenant with you.*

So when Ephesians 3:6 says that we are "partakers of the promise in Christ Jesus through the gospel" the full benefit comes from truly knowing *which* promise you gain. The quality of your spiritual life depends on the identity you adopt relative to the *promise* you are given, the *adoption* you walk in, the *faith* you possess, and the *rest* you enjoy.

You have been bought with a great price (1 Cor. 6:19-20). You are no longer your own. The most violent, powerful force for love in the universe has personally committed Himself to your absolute well-being! You said yes to Him, *good!* Far more sobering, liberating, captivating and anchoring *is the unshakeable fact that He said yes to you.* He has taken you at your word, and now taken over. This is the secret to the perseverance of the saints, that God Himself is faithful to His covenant to cause those that are HIs to persevere to the end, faithful and true (Jude 1:24, John 17:12,17). We must think like sons of the (New) Covenant or we will never be more than Heaven-bound orphans.

READY TO
VANISH AWAY

**"In speaking of a new covenant, he makes
the first one obsolete. And what is
becoming obsolete and growing old is
ready to vanish away" (Heb. 8:10).**

A t the start of this booklet I included a lengthy quotation
from Hebrews chapter 8. It would benefit you to pause,
go back, and ponder again why the ministry of Christ contains
"better promises" than the Law of Moses — oh, how much
better! — concluding, in fact, with a promise that was actually
impossible under the Law: that God will be merciful not to our
righteousness, but our unrighteousness. By contrast, the Law
required dreadful curses be laid upon the unrighteous. Since all
men were constantly unrighteous and frequently rebellious, the
history of Israel is rife with curses being frequently enacted
upon individuals, as well as the entire nation. Such sins were
only temporarily atoned for by the sacrificial system, also
provided for by the Law.

We readily receive our "better promise" at salvation as the work of God in "forgiving our wickedness" (NLT) — past tense — yet promptly forget those promises over the course of our sanctification process whenever we fail God or yield to sin, especially habitual sin. Yet the promise has not changed, only our confidence in it. Why does that happen? Why are we shaken? In Christ, the promise is actually perpetual — this is part of the "better" feature list. It requires no further action but faith on our part. (James makes clear that works *will* follow faith, but that is a different conversation). By contrast, the Law required constant maintenance and additional sacrifice, and still never really fulfilled the purpose of producing righteous inner conformity — heart level affection, submission, and trust — toward the Lord. This is why the Law was:

- only for a time (Gal. 3:17-25, Heb. 8:7, 9:10)
- of strict and limited purpose (1 Tim. 1:9, Rom. 7:5, 7)
- entirely unsuccessful in transforming man (Heb. 7:19, 9:9, Rom. 8:3)
- equally unsuccessful in truly uniting man to God (Heb. 7:18-19, 8:13)

If we do not understand the present, perpetual grace of the New Covenant, we may not understand grace at all because it is only by understanding the covenantal mind of God that we can understand the radical, endless grace Christ offers. Only here, in the full force of the unmixed New Covenant, will the Accuser truly be silenced in our lives.

I have a number of study bibles. The Orthodox Study Bible has a great summary of the central contrast between old and new:

> "Christ's covenant solves the problems that Moses' could not. Both covenants come from God's grace and require man's willed response. However, Moses' covenant (1) is external to man and cannot solve the root of man's problem, sin and death; (2) cannot reunite and reintegrate man's soul; (3) is learned by teaching; (4) is heeded with fearful compliance; and (5) gives imperfect forgiveness. Christ's covenant (1) is internal—it heals our nature; (2) unifies the inner man—heart and mind are joined in union with God; (3) is therefore grasped intuitively; (4) is heeded with willing cooperation (synergy); and (5) gives perfect forgiveness, even of those sins the old covenant was powerless to deal with."

While this provides a useful summary, it does not address the central problem of sin, nor the hope of righteousness. Righteousness can be a fuzzy concept. We get it in a moment of revelation and grace, but then it slips away as law-thinking creeps back in. In this, Abraham shines as the premiere example of the type of righteousness God seeks, and it is for this reason that Abraham is called, "The Father of our Faith".

> **"For what does the Scripture say? 'Abraham *believed* God, and *it was counted to him as***

> *righteousness.'* **Now to the one who works, his wages are not counted as a gift but as his due. And to the one who does not work but believes in him who justifies the ungodly, his faith is counted as righteousness" (Rom. 4:3-5).**

The reason righteousness can feel so fuzzy and hard to grasp, so elusive that it slips away in moments of weakness, sin, and failure leaving us guilt-ridden and striving in the flesh, is because we aren't exactly sure what defines righteousness to begin with! It is actually quite simple, as this legal, relational framework will demonstrate: The core theological concept behind righteousness is that a person is either in "right standing" with God, or they are not. Easy, right? Now let's add a couple of definitions to remove ambiguity. We want righteousness and that means right standing. But what determines right standing?

- • <u>Righteousness</u> = "Right Standing" = "The qualitative and relational status determined by fidelity to the terms of God's covenant."

- • <u>Simplified</u>: "Righteousness is obedience to the terms of the covenant."

In short, perhaps you now realize why it is critical to know which covenant you are under! Furthermore, *you get to choose,* i.e. the manner in which you "achieve" righteousness is the ultimate act of your own free will. You can produce righteousness with disciplined, perfectly consistent choices and actions of supreme moral virtue in full compliance with the Law of Moses, or by faith, you can allow God to impart His righteousness to you, totally unearned and undeserved. Like Abraham, you *believe* God, and *it gets counted to you as righteousness.*

Both are ways of relating to God. You can relate under the terms of an Old Covenant or a New Covenant. Either way, you choose! As a Christian, day by day, you *still must choose.* This is why Paul reminded the Colossians, "Therefore, *as you received Christ Jesus* the Lord, *so walk in him*, rooted and built up in him and *established in the faith*" (Col. 2:6-7). In other words, how did you enter relationship with Christ? By grace, through faith.

There is no other way. That's the deal. That's the terms of the New Covenant. "For by grace you have been saved through faith. And this is not your own doing; it is the gift of God, not a result of works, so that no one may boast (Eph. 2:8-9).

You can't add to it, He did it *all*. You don't supply any righteousness, you draw on His. You don't add any virtue or goodness. Quite the opposite, you bring your failures, shame and sin! He adds His virtue and goodness. He alone is the spotless lamb.

How did you receive Him? Did you find Him, or did He find you? Did you do well, or did He lavish mercy? We begin by grace through faith, we continue by grace through faith. Any subtle shift toward works or self-dependence is drifting from the Lord.

As you once *received*, keep receiving…so *walk*.

- Rooted in love (Eph. 3:17-19)
- Built up with gifts (1 Cor. 14:3, 26)
- Established in faith (Col. 2:7)
- Abounding in thanksgiving (Col. 2:7)

We are rooted and built up in Him, not by works, effort, or performance. This is how we walk. Or is it?

"Hey, how is your walk, brother?"

"Well, I haven't fallen in three days. I'm reading my Bible, but I'm not praying like I should. I'm not thankful enough. I kicked my dog in anger, etc."

No, no, no! That's old thinking: old man, Old Covenant, old righteousness. The writer of Hebrews points to that and says it is obsolete, growing old, and ready to vanish away.

The *new* way, the *new* covenant, the *better* promise, is this:

You are "rooted and built up in Him."

"So how is your walk, brother?"

"God is so faithful!" you reply. "I've stumbled, but He keeps talking to me and loving me. I can't *do* anything that makes me righteous, but that was never the point. I can only grow in His righteousness. He is showing me that I can be His friend even in my weakness. One day at at time!"

Amen.

THE PERIL OF
GOD'S NEARNESS

**"You cannot see My face, for no man can
see Me and live!" (Exo. 33:20)**

God desires fellowship. Man needs God to live. But in Exodus 33, to see God is to die. Obviously, this poses a real conundrum to fellowship, both on the human side, and the divine. We are left with a troubling, ironic question.

How do you survive God?

Hopefully by now you will pause and consider whether you are about to give an Old Covenant answer or a New Covenant answer. In this chapter and the next, we will examine the historical narrative recorded in Scripture by which this problem manifested.

For now, set this dilemma in the middle of a population center. Imagine stashing an armed thermonuclear bomb in a canvas tent in the middle of a chaotic refugee camp occupied by 3 million people, any one of whom could wander into the tent and accidentally detonate it? This is not far from the dangerous scenario created by God's loving commitment to dwell among His people.

God's tangible presence in the midst of Israel was the absolute best thing for them, but the danger His presence posed to the very people He loved was quite real. How do we reconcile the irony? What happened, especially since Scripture emphatically shows that from the very beginning God *always* wanted to dwell among humans?

Fellowship was the purpose of Creation. God called it good! The Garden of Eden was a designed environment. It was neither an aberration, nor a tease. It was supposed to be normal.

Walking with God, fellowshipping with Him, was intended *by God* as "normal human life."

Tragically, sin made a mess of that. Right from the start.

But God didn't quit. He faithfully continued working generally and universally with all humans for a time until two back-to-back incidents, the Great Flood and the Tower of Babel, proved that all humans generally preferred rebellion to obedience.

So God changed tactics.

He narrowed His plan to one family. When a man named Abram from the Chaldean region of Ur responded positively to Yahweh's invitation to trust and fellowship together by faith, God singled him out by instituting a covenant of grace and blessing that would extend from Abraham to all his descendants forever. Mind you, this covenant contained no curse for Abraham (only for Abraham's enemies)! All nations would *eventually* be blessed through this covenant, but an important historical footnote is that the Jew-Gentile divide began here.

This is an important detail because for thousands of years to come God would narrow His direct involvement, His purpose, His focus, and His self-revelation, to Abraham's family alone. The legacy of this is secondarily seen in the matchless gift of divinely inspired oracles first entrusted to Jewish prophets, historians and writers. Only through the infallible Word of God can we know God on His own terms, free of the sort of dangerous, manmade contaminations that infect every other religious system. Those truths were entirely entrusted to Abraham's extended family.

However, the primary gift of Abraham's line is Jesus Himself. The Messiah of all nations is a Jew. The long prophesied answer of God to the problem of sin came from Abraham's seed and none other.

That's not to say that it was an easy road. Rather, it was quite bumpy and convoluted at times. God sovereignly used all of it redemptively, even the worst parts, yet the plot would twist and turn many, many times before the true plan of God could finally be fully revealed *and* understood. In fact, to this day many Christians still do not understand the real point of the story! Here's part of the warning of history we often miss:

Abraham's family did *not* stay in Abraham's *faith,* with vast and negative consequences.

History as Object Lesson

This requires further explanation. If I am successful, you will see the history of Israel in a different light than you were probably taught in Sunday School. Driven to Egypt, Abraham's family multiplied into a great nation, but 400 years of slavery molded the nation's hope and expectations—their identity—to Pharaoh's cruel bondage more than the legacy of their founding fathers. Since God's promise to Abraham was eternal, He brought them out in due time. Israel's exodus from Egypt was dramatic in the extreme, attended by great signs of power designed to demonstrate beyond all doubt Yahweh's great love for Abraham's descendants. Over and over God's favorable actions on Israel's behalf are attributed to His unending faithfulness to the covenant He made with his friend centuries before (Isaiah 41:8).

In fact, when God was set to destroy Israel after the Golden Calf incident, saying, "Now therefore let me alone, that my wrath may burn hot against them and I may consume them" Moses did not appeal to God's merciful nature, but to His history of covenantal friendship established by the original three generations of faith.

"*Remember* Abraham, Isaac and Jacob," Moses pleads. "Don't destroy the offspring of our righteous ancestors. Instead, forgive their descendants simply because of their pedigree" (Exodus 32:10-14).

Even today, Jews call this '*zekhut 'avot*,' the merit of the ancestors. But what was their merit? "And he (Abram) *believed* the LORD, and he *counted it to him as righteousness*" (Genesis 15:6, italics mine).

So if God relented because of Abraham's faith, the question must be asked, how did Israel fall so far, so fast, as to get to that dreadful point of idolatry and judgment in the first place?

The Cost of Unbelief

Centuries after Abraham, Isaac, and Jacob, the fledgling slave nation of Israel failed the trial of faith in the wilderness. This happened long before the negative report of the twelve spies and the punishment of forty years of wandering. Nor was it a single failure, but a sequence of failures at a heart level over several weeks following their deliverance from Egypt.

What do I mean? Read the progression from the exodus liberation event through a series of trust challenges, finally culminating at Massah and Meribah (Exo. 17:1-7, Num. 20:13, Psa. 106:22-23, 95:7-8, Heb. 4:7) and you will see how Israel corporately moved from immature complaining to deep-seated accusation against the fundamental goodness of the very same God who so dramatically and providentially rescued them in the first place.

In short, Israel abandoned the faith of their father Abraham, defined as a persistent expectation of goodness and promises fulfilled. Instead, they viewed God as a trickster, homicidal deity who actually intended to kill them, even though all He had done to that point was save, heal, provide, and deliver. As a result, at Sinai, they were offered a new deal, and they took it. They exchanged the extraordinary birthright of their Abrahamic blessing by agreeing to the terms of a replacement covenant proposed by God by which they would relate to God only based on the merit of their performance.

This is the absolutely worst trade-in-value, bad-lemon-car-deal of all time! After all, God had done mighty things, moved greatly on their behalf, and shown a continual forbearing spirit to their fears and insecurities in the early days and weeks of the Exodus.

But they simply refused to believe His fundamental intention toward them was good. In response, God stipulated the terms of a different covenant. This covenant admittedly included massive Abrahamic-style benefits, but also, as a first for Abraham's children, terrifying curses and negative consequences as a result of any moral failure or disobedience. The covenant would be negotiated by Moses on behalf of the people, and it would interpose with priority above Abraham's covenant in how God would continue relating to Israel in the future.

If you read the terms of that covenant given in Leviticus 26:1-46 and Deuteronomy 28:1-30:20, you will see that the space given to delineating the curses is more than double the space given to the blessings!

You have to understand something. God is not schizophrenic. He is not a different God here or there. He is the same God acting with total faithfulness to the terms of different covenants. Until Sinai, Abraham's children were living under

Abraham. After Sinai, they were living under Moses. Until Christ, we were *all* under Moses, which meant we were all condemned to death and spiritual separation from God. Now we are under Christ.

Indeed, mercifully and thankfully, the rules have changed.

But here's the deal: it doesn't matter if don't *know* it...and we don't, or at least we all-too-easily lose it from one moment to the next. We have to know that Christ came to both restore and surpass the privileges of Abraham's blessing to all who would likewise act in faith, both Jew and Gentile, while also bearing the full penalty of satisfying the curse which every generation, born and unborn, invoked by our collective failure to comply with the letter of the Law received at Sinai.

Plainly stated, the Pact at Sinai was a covenant of performance, not a covenant of grace. In itself, that point is not greatly controversial. What would be controversial is to assert that the Pact of Sinai might have been optional and that Israel may have chosen poorly in saying yes to it. Nevertheless, I believe there is Biblical grounds to believe that is, indeed, the case.

In an ironic twist, we must even see that God's threat in Exodus 33 — "no man can see me and live" — chronologically did not occur until the Sinai Pact was ratified (which happened in Chapter 24). God revealed Himself to Abraham face-to-face without peril in Genesis 18.[1]

Though sin was fatal to body and spirit, right relationship with God was always possible by faith (even if only in token form until Christ would be revealed).

RECOVERING THE
PATH OF FAITH

"Listen to me, *you who pursue*
righteousness . . . look to the rock from
which you were hewn. *Look to Abraham*
your father" (Isa. 51:1-2a)

D o you want to live righteously? Good! No wonder we are
instructed to look to Abraham, not Moses. So why do
discussions of holiness most often start with what we are
supposed to *do,* rather than believe? Often missed in this
discussion is that righteousness by faith was *always* possible,
beginning with Abel (Heb. 11:4). Abraham chose the better
path, and so must we. Greatly simplified, here's the story:

We start with Abraham, who chose the Faith Path; God
rewarded him and his descendants with an eternal covenant

   —> By default, Israel was still under this covenant when
        they departed Egypt, but soon proved they would not
        live (or abide) under it.

———>   In its place, God gave them a Works Path, a rule-based covenant that bound them to obedience as much as they had previously been bound to Pharaoh. In fact, the bondage of the Law was meant to dramatically confirm that they could never improve themselves enough to be considered righteous. Thus, the entire sacrificial system was structured to be a continual reminder of its own insufficiency by only temporarily atoning for human sin.

"The sacrifices under that system were repeated again and again . . . but they were *never able to provide perfect cleansing* . . . If they could have provided perfect cleansing, the sacrifices would have stopped, for the worshipers would have been purified once for all time, *and their feelings of guilt would have disappeared.* But *instead, those sacrifices actually reminded them of their sins* year after year . . . That is why . . . Christ came into the world" (Hebrews 10:1-5a, NLT)

————>   Thus, in the fulness of time, Christ was *"born of woman, born under the law, to redeem those who were under the law, so that we might receive adoption as sons"* – Galatians 4:4-5. In other words, from inside the system, Jesus drew humanity into Himself so He could bring us outside the system (just like Moses entering Egypt to bring Israel out). The death and resurrection of Jesus put a historical bookend on the controlling influence of the Law as God's primary measurement of righteousness. The Law still exists, perfect and righteous, and righteousness is still required if we wish to relate to God. But the Law is no longer the means of *achieving* or *sustaining* righteousness for those who relate to God's gracious provision in Christ.

As Paul revealed to the Galatians, to live under the dictates of the Law is to live as an orphan before God, exactly the opposite of what the Father desires for His children. "Law Christians" persist in a mindset of slavery *because a slave's only value or sense of accomplishment is to be a good worker.* The source of many struggling Christians' constant striving, competitiveness, fear and shame is often not what preacher's target — a deficiency of their personal resolve or dedication to God — but rather in the covenant they have chosen to live under!

Furthermore, if I have to work to please God, then I also have to work to keep Him pleased with me more than you, or my status and self-worth will feel threatened. If I live as an orphan and another orphan is doing better than me, I will find no joy in your success. My soul is ever in anguish, defeated either by my failure or your triumph. On those rare moments that I succeed, I cannot truly enjoy it because my small triumph now becomes a precious prize I must guard and grow. To maintain my status, I must be vigilant and never let my guard down. I return to my laundry list of dos and don'ts because I think those rules will help me keep my laundry clean, forgetting that all my righteousness remains as filthy rags. I am not secure in God, I am insecure because I am in myself. Orphan souls live in a zero-sum game of limited resources under a stern taskmaster ("bake bricks without straw!" Exodus 5:18). Always inhaling, never exhaling. Never experiencing true rest.

Til one day, on a bloody hill and a cursed tree, love broke through.

Since that day, as you travel life's roads, God has closed the complex network of toll booths designed to finance the cost of sin. He declared the entire sin management system bankrupt. God is no longer in the business of relating to sin, He relates to faith. He speaks truth. He empowers righteousness. And He deals with us through the currency of grace.

Choose You This Day

Once upon a time, in your natural life, you were born naked and screaming under sin, law and death. To come under the blood of Jesus is to be born *again* into abundant life. Where you were once dead in sin, you have now been made alive in Christ! (Romans 6:11). However, that verse requires that you continually act on this truth to stay in this truth. You must "*consider yourself* dead to sin and alive to God" (italics mine).

Not dead *in* sin, but *to* sin. Not alive in yourself, but to God, on His terms. By His power.

Do you struggle with sin? Do you feel like a sinner? Do you feel alive? This is no longer a reasonable question, as your feelings have nothing to do with it. That's why you can live in a truth, but not experience its benefits. In fact, truth is just a doorway to freedom; you must choose whether you will enter it regardless of how you feel. Since you can only possess what you experience, how do you *consider* yourself: 1) according to the Word, 2) according to your circumstance, or 3) according to your feelings? Hint: two of those are wrong answers.

In other words, like Israel, freshly delivered from Egypt, you must continually choose where you will abide. Daily, you must walk in faith. Daily, you must depend on His righteousness, not your own. Daily, you must receive the gift He offers. If you began in grace, you must settle that you could never finish without it. You awaken each day in a temple marked by blood.

Do you wish to live as an indebted orphan or as emancipated, adopted, blood-kin? As a slave with no inherent privileges, or as a grateful son or daughter possessing full inheritance? The gift has been given and the debt has been paid. All that remains is the terrible, glorious burden of choosing where you will live: Old Covenant or New?

You are on a journey from Egypt to the Promised Land. As your will is slowly being conformed to His, you will no doubt fail along the way. Settle failure as a businessman might estimate cost of goods sold, as part of the overhead of life. I did not say *excuse* failure, or dismiss moral weakness, I merely confirmed that struggles, failures and suffering are part of your journey toward inheritance. In the end, you are meant to overcome. Along the way you will have many victories and many setbacks, but no one enters the Promised Land until they learn the ways of faith. Will you stay in Christ, at rest, or will you for guilt or shame head to Sinai and try to relieve your guilt, do penance, sacrifice something to prove your worth to God?

From antiquity through the late 19th century, the primitive practice of "bloodletting" was the most common curative performed by surgeons for nearly 2000 years. Bleeding a person to cure their sickness was such a picture of our deeply felt need to bleed appropriately, but the lesson seems never to be learned: your sacrifice of blood can never restore you, only His.

In light of this, the question is not whether you *will* fail, but how will you respond to your failure. It will test with you uncertainty and fear. It will beg you to *do* something. You must begin to recognize the difference between the voice of the Spirit and the prompting of the Law. The more you try to contain, justify, or explain away the failure, the more relentlessly the Law will provoke that sin to manifest itself (Romans 7). The only answer is to live by the Spirit for therein lies the promise that "you will not gratify the desires of the flesh" (Galatians 5:16).

Outside of the Cross of Christ, every human religion is an attempt to beat this system by mastering it, but it's not possible and *that's the point!* A perfect code of perfect performance based on perfect virtue is *only natural to God, not humanity.* We can never work our way into that status. If we are to become holy, it can only be at His instigation, by His design, and by His supply.

We have a word for that divine supply: grace.

> **"Where sin increased, grace abounded all the more, so that . . . <u>grace also might reign through righteousness</u>"** (Romans 5:20-21)

Grace is not a way to get you off the hook, it is primarily power to overcome. It faces sin, consumes it, buries it in mercy, then releases spiritual adrenaline to reign over it with righteousness in future encounters. It does this by assuring us of the *present* righteousness of Christ at work in our lives before the sin, during the sin, and after whatever sinful deed temporarily knocks you out. Yes, you read that right: grace is present during the sin. God does not lift His gift of grace when we struggle, which means He does not lift His gift of righteousness when we fail. To do so would be conditional, which is Law, not grace. Grace is unconditional.

PERFECTED
FOR ALL TIME

"For whoever keeps the whole law but fails
in one point has become *guilty of all* of it."
(James 2:10)

L aw says you fail, you fall, you pay. Law says fellowship is
broken until payment is made, with each payment being
proven by a fresh sacrifice of new resolve and deep repentance
in your soul. But the writer of Hebrews paints a far different
picture of what Christ achieved on the Cross, both in the
singularity of the achievement and the permanence of its effect,
thereby redefining the terms of fellowship with God at every
stage of our journey.

"We *have been sanctified* through the offering of
the body of Jesus Christ *once for all* . . . For by a *single
offering* he has *perfected for all time* those who *are
being sanctified*" (Hebrews 10:10-14)

This is a radical statement. It's almost unbelievable, and that's the problem Most don't believe, or don't live like they do. But there it is: you *are* sanctified and *have been* made perfect, even while you *are still being* sanctified. Furthermore, your offering has nothing to do with it. His offering is all that matters and He has already offered all. Once for all. That means the game of endless sacrifices is over. That system is no longer in effect.

If you simply get what you deserve, the New Covenant is not so new, and the Good News is not so good. It may be true religious news, but it is not good news. In fact, that kind of Christianity is closer to Karma than Christ. Robert Farrar Capon puts it this way:

> **"Grace is the celebration of life, relentlessly hounding all the non-celebrants in the world. It is a floating, cosmic bash shouting its way through the streets of the universe, flinging the sweetness of its cassations to every window, pounding at every door in a hilarity beyond all liking and happening, until the prodigals come out at last and dance, and the elder brothers finally take their fingers out of their ears . . . Grace cannot prevail . . . until our lifelong certainty that someone is keeping score has run out of steam and collapsed."[2]**

The opposite of capital 'S' Sin is not Virtue, as we suppose, no matter how much the inner compulsions of Law attempt to make us think otherwise, as if by chasing Virtue we could find the antidote to Sin. Don't fault Law for this failing, for that is its intended strength! The entire purpose of the Law is to do just that: define perfect Virtue so relentlessly you give up to ever achieve it on your own. Then what? What fills that gap? How do you climb out of that hole?

You can't. You can only believe for a miracle.

Thus, the opposite of Sin is not Virtue but Faith, and Faith has nothing to do with Law. The danger for most Christians is to come to Christ by grace, then slowly, imperceptibly wander away, missing and forgetting the rhythm of grace in their walk. This will actually keep them in a position of never being empowered for the holiness they seek since . . .

> ". . . **the grace of God has appeared** (why?) . . . *training us to renounce ungodliness* **and** *worldly passions,* **and to** *live self-controlled, upright, and godly lives* **in the present age (Titus 2:11-12)**

Do you want to live holy before God? You don't need less grace, or to guard yourself from the excesses of grace. You need gushing buckets of grace! But this is not our message. For generations, our discipleship has mainly consisted of impressing upon people the burden of holiness to such a degree that they leave the revival meeting appropriately filled with self-loathing at how poorly they have lived up to the standard of God, determined to make a better sacrifice in the future. Our only option, we are routinely taught, is to fulfill the Law or God will be displeased, and so with renewed vigor, we open our veins and give all our passion and strength to doing better. This is spiritual bloodletting.

Beloved, if that is your walk with God, you're doomed. You may be saved and bound for heaven, but you're doomed to despair and defeat on earth.

The work of the Law is to assure your failure to such a degree that every time you think you can beat it, and fail, you will be pushed back into dependence on Christ. In the end, the Law itself confirms that Law-based righteousness is a bad idea. Why? Because it is a totally unsustainable system upon which to base human righteousness, therefore it is totally unsustainable for keeping humans in confident fellowship with their Heavenly Father.

This is why the writer of Hebrews urges us to "leave the elementary doctrine of Christ and go on to maturity, not laying again a foundation of repentance from dead works" (Heb. 6:1).

The work is done. Kaput. You have nothing to add to it except your faith and gratitude. Jesus said, "It is finished." Believe it! Quite trying to re-repent. Instead, now it is time to…

"Trust him. And when you have done that, you are living the life of grace. No matter what happens to you in the course of that trusting – no matter how

many waverings you may have, no matter how many suspicions that you have bought a poke with no pig in it, no matter how much heaviness and sadness your lapses, vices, indispositions, and bratty whining may cause you – you believe simply that Somebody Else, by his death and resurrection, has made it all right, and you just say thank you and shut up. The whole slop-closet full of mildewed performances (which is all you have to offer) is simply your death; it is Jesus who is your life. If he refused to condemn you because your works were rotten, he certainly isn't going to flunk you because your faith isn't so hot. You can fail utterly, therefore, and still live the life of grace. You can fold up spiritually, morally, or intellectually and still be safe. Because at the very worst, all you can be is dead – and for him who is the Resurrection and the Life, that just makes you his cup of tea." 3

3 MAJOR COVENANTS: CONTRAST & OVERVIEW

A s we have seen, Abraham was the full beneficiary of God's unconditional favor expressed through a Covenant of Grace. He received this benefit by faith, not works. In fact, shockingly, this covenant contained no curse for Abraham or his offspring...*only* blessings. Curses were reserved by God for Abraham's enemies.

Think of that — a pretty good deal for sure!

However, as we near the end, because these are likely such new concepts I am going to insert an overview of the contrasting components of each of the three major covenants for your further study. I've supplied a few Scriptures with each, though many more could be given. These truths are expounded upon in much greater detail in Course One, but if you aren't ready to take the full course, I want to give you plenty to chew on. To that end, I hope you find this framework useful.

Abraham's Covenant = FAITH (Rom. 4:20-22)
- Timing: Perpetual (Gal. 3:15)
- Responsibility: God, unilateral

The Total Superiority of the New Covenant

- Terms: First, believe. As evidence, later, be circumcised. (Rom. 4:11-12)
- Relationship: To God, directly, but externally; foreshadowing.
- Produces: A son, favor, no curse

Moses's Covenant = LAW (Gal. 3:10-12)

- Timing: Intermediary, parallel, temporary (Gal. 3:17, 19, 23-25; Heb. 8:13)
- Responsibility: Both men and God, bilateral
- Terms: Obey every part of the code with total fidelity. Failure to any degree, even accidental, brings guilt and judgment (Deut. 11:13-17, 26-28, 27:26; 2 Chron. 24:20; Ezek. 18:4-9; Gal. 3:10).
- Note 1: the complications: James 2:10 says, "For whoever keeps the whole law and yet stumbles at just one point is guilty of breaking *all* of it." In other words, *it doesn't matter how much you do right, the part you do wrong will condemn you.* This creates an un-winnable scenario for sustained blessing and positive relationship, which is God's desire as our Father. Also, this explains divine "fickleness" passages, since the terms of this covenant are conditional based on behavior/performance. (Isa. 2:6, 54:7; Jer. 3:8; Psa. 44:23; Amos 2:4; esp. Eze. 16, 20:13-38).
- Note 2: God's "perseverance" during constant cycles of Law-breaking was not based on Law (the Law itself

permitted divorce!). Rather, God's resolve came *from His perpetual fidelity to Abraham* Psa. 105:8-9, which thereby precipitated the future certainty of the Eternal Covenant. The superior promise of God to Abraham, Isaac and Jacob became the basis for Moses (the Law) to appeal to God's unfailing mercy and steadfast love, such that even Israel's violation of the conditional covenant made at Sinai (Exo.19. 5-6) would not justify destroying Israel.

- Relationship: Not to God, but Law, as intermediary and proxy for God; veiled. (2 Cor. 3:14-15)
- Produces: Servants, blessing, cursing (Deut. 28:1-30:20)

Christ's Covenant = Completion of Abraham's (Rom. 4:13-16, 23-24; Gal. 3:14, 29) = FAITH (Rom. 3:21-2; Gal. 3:11)

- Timing: Eternal (Isa. 54:9-10, 14-15; Eze. 11:19, 36:26; Jer. 31:33)
- Responsibility: God, unilateral (Rom. 8:3-4)
- Terms: Believe and receive (Rom. 1:17, Gal. 2:16-17)
- Relationship: To God, directly, internally; indwelt, unveiled. (2 Cor. 3:16-18)
- Produces : Sonship, spirit of adoption (Rom. 8:14-16), favor and blessing, and no curse (Rom. 7:4, 6, 8:1-2), clean conscience (Heb. 9:14, 10:2; 1 John 3:20)

Do not miss this critical point. By faith, we are *not* under Moses any longer, but we can still live like we are. *Our daily mindset can still be submitted in fear to Moses.* If so, we are living a beggar's life in great neglect of the costly sacrifice of Jesus.

Mind you, Christ does not replace, discount, ignore, or cheat the Law. No, no…He completely encompasses it. It is only by fulfilling it *for* us that He can legally make it obsolete *to* us with all its demands, penalties and requirements. Therefore, *righteousness* (and with it, a clean conscience and unending favor), are not produced by good works or—listen carefully!— even obedience, but *faith*. Only faith (Gal. 4:13-16). We can have this confidence because those are the terms of the New Covenant clearly spelled out in Scripture. You can live under the terms of the old if you choose, but *why* would you when *the new is totally superior?*

> **"For Christ is the end of the law *for righteousness* to everyone who *believes*" (Rom. 10:4).**

Note, the Law has not ended. May it never be, for then God would cease to be altogether righteous! Rather, in Christ, the Law no longer has any bearing on how the Father relates to you. He does not measure or determine our personal righteousness by Law, but by the presence or absence of His Son within us.

Do you *believe* in Jesus Christ?

If so, your righteousness is no longer measured by your fulfillment of the Law, but by His.

COVENANT TERMS
Understanding the Difference

	Abraham (Rom. 4:20-22) – FAITH – GRACE	Moses (Gal. 3:10-12) – LAW – PERFORMANCE	Christ (Heb. 9:15) – FAITH – GRACE
Timing	PERPETUAL (Gal. 3:15)	PARALLEL (Gal. 3:17, 19, 23-25)	ETERNAL (Isa. 54; Eze. 36; Jer. 31)
Parties Responsible	UNILATERAL God alone	BILATERAL God & Man	UNILATERAL God alone (Rom. 8:3-4)
Legal Terms	BELIEVE Later, as evidence, be circumcised.	OBEY Total fidelity to the code. Failure invokes judgment.	BELIEVE & RECEIVE Grace through Faith (Eph. 2:8-9)
Relationship	TO GOD, directly. Friendship, external	TO LAW as God-proxy (2 Cor. 3:14-15), ext., veiled.	TO GOD, directly internal, indwelt, unveiled
Yield	SON favor, no curse	SLAVES with blessing, cursing (Deut. 28:1-30:20)	SONSHIP, Spirit of adoption, favor (Rom. 8:14-16). Curse broken.
Unconditional	✓	no	✓

The Total Superiority of the New Covenant

CONFIDENT LIFE, NO MORE CURSE

"For *all who rely on works of the law are under a curse*; for it is written, "Cursed be everyone who does not abide by all things written in the Book of the Law, and do them." Now it is evident that *no one is justified before God by the law*, for "The righteous shall live by faith." But the law is not of faith, rather "The *one who does them shall live* by them" (Gal. 3:10-12).

I don't want to live under a curse, do you? Law, by definition, is about what I *do*, not what I believe. But that leads to a curse, because I inevitably *do* it wrong. If history tells us anything, it tells us that people, cultures, and nations do it wrong. This is a universal truth. It is called the sin nature. If avoiding wrongdoing is my focus, now I am focused on sin itself, not God. Do you see the irony? So if I come to God by grace for the sake of salvation, then proceed to live the outworking of my sanctification *in dependence on the Law to justify myself*, I expose myself, in practical terms, to the consequences of a different covenant. I can be a New Covenant believer living as an Old Covenant Christian.

When the Galatians started doing this, Paul was angry and perplexed. He asked a series of probing questions.

> **"Who has bewitched you?...Did you receive the Spirit by works of the law or by hearing with faith? Are you so foolish? Having begun by the Spirit, are you now being perfected by the flesh?" (Gal. 3:1-3)**

You can't come to Christ and then fall back to Law, yet in the mix of life's complexities, pressures, circumstances, doubts, bad (but sincere) discipleship training, and faulty foundations, we do it all the time. Our paradigm slips, and our faith slips with it. Staying in the peace and grace of the New Covenant takes practice, renewal, confession, and much, much washing with the water of the Word.

Remember, Law is conditional. *Do this* and God will be with you. *Fail* and you are cursed (Dan. 9:11). Your failure could be so great that His presence might even depart. This is the nature of the Law. It's what Israel agreed to. By contrast, the covenant with Abraham was unconditional. God's oath to the patriarchs was to give them countless descendants and eternal possession of the promised land (Gen. 12:7; 13:15-16; 15:5; 17:7-8). It was unilateral, unconditional, and irrevocable (Gen. 17:7; Deut. 4:31).

No wonder that when push came to shove, Moses did not try in Exodus 32-33 to convince God that Israel could improve or reform. He simply reminded God of the faith of his forefathers (see Deut 7:12 for a single verse summary) and of God's promise to them. The relational equity of Abraham, Isaac, and Jacob with God became the basis by which Moses (representing Law itself!) could appeal to God's unfailing mercy and steadfast love, even though the newly ratified, conditional covenant terms of Sinai (Exo.19. 5-6) would have justified Him entirely in destroying Israel. Because Moses appealed to *Abraham's standing before God*, God relented.

That faith is and always has been the basis of true righteousness. It is why we are meant to abide in Christ with total peace, confidence, and hope—because the conditions and the curse of the Law are nullified so that we now abide in the unconditional love of Christ who "will never leave us or forsake us." The work of Christ is so vast, so complete, the half has not been told. It stretches in every direction, targeting every curse. Every Christmas we sing a famous line from Beethoven's classical masterpiece, *Joy to the World:* "He (Jesus) comes to make His blessings flow, far as the curse is found"

Thus, as we draw this booklet to a close, I urge you to let the totality of the cross become re-plumbed in your soul and spirit with fresh revelation. My main goal is contained in the title, to communicate to your heart the *total* superiority of the New Covenant, and thereby call us all back to a radical, unmixed commitment to life under it, not Law. Why would we ever want to return to cold adherence to code rather than to live in relationship with God in the beauty, kindness, truth and empowering work of the Holy Spirit?

We must not grow dull to the singular terror, wretchedness, and majesty of this lonely, bloody day, by which all history and eternity are marked. Jesus said, "It is finished!" *and He meant it.* The cross is the devastating beachhead of redemption by which the Lord of Lords invades history to take back for us the ground which Adam forfeited. We do not yet live in the totality of it, for there must also be a process of renewal and appropriation, an overcoming tenacity, a progressive faith, filling of the Spirit, and glorification to come. But the cross stands forever as the anchor point upon which all of the enemy's rage, power, and wisdom were brought to ruin, and the weight and penalty of sin (guilt, emotional torment, mental confusion, physical infirmity, rebellion, pride, vice) were brought to their proper, shameful end in His body.

The cross is thus the fulcrum upon which all of history pivots, and the work of Christ on the Cross is eternally complete. There is nothing to add to it because absolutely nothing *can* be added to it. Every vestige of the curse is addressed at Calvary; therefore, every blessing now can flow.

Understanding this means we must recognize: Jesus did not merely *take* the curse in a generalized (albeit total) sense. No, He *became...your* curse. At this level, redemption is not cosmic and abstract victory, it is profoundly practical and highly personal.

The Total Superiority of the New Covenant

How far, how wide, how deep does the curse bleed into my human experience, failures, choices, and fears? However and wherever I find its stain, there I find a bleeding man on a cross. He hangs there for a reason. Would I cut short his favor, his gift, his pain, through unbelief? Salvation and heaven, fine. Yes, thanks. But "*this* and *this* and *this!*" we protest in unbelief, seeing our sin as larger than His love. Under the Old Covenant, you cannot help but think that way. It is time for us to grow up into fulness and see our pitiful works-based living for what it is. That kind of thinking is part of the curse, not the Kingdom.

Under the new deal, freely offered, freely received, life is, well...*new.* Open your eyes!

The New Covenant of Life in Christ is superior in every way to the Law of Moses for nurturing relationship with God and producing righteousness in the inner man.

On the next page, see the chart, "20 Distinctions."
Get access to the 58-session video course (10 hrs) @
DeanBriggs.com/courses

The Total Superiority of the New Covenant

WELCOME TO LIFE

IN THE NEW COVENANT!

20 DISTINCTIONS BETWEEN LAW AND GRACE

#	LAW	GRACE
1	Demands total compliance, curses failure Deut. 28:15, 45; Dan. 9:11	Satisfies holy demand, removes guilt & shame Rom 8:1
2	Condemns & kills Rom 7:9-11	Justifies and heals Rom. 7:24, 8:3-4,6,11
3	Says, "Do & Don't" Exo. 20:7-17	Says, "Done" John 17:4
4	Curses Gal. 3:10	Blesses Gal. 3:14
5	Destroys sinners Lev. 24:14-16; Deut. 17:5	Makes sinners alive Rom 8:2
6	Says, "Be holy until you are" Lev. 11:44-45	Says, "It is finished" John 19:30
7	Condemns even the best man James 2:10; Gal. 3:10; John 3:3	Saves even the worst man 1 Tim 1:15
8	Says, "Pay all that you owe" Mat. 18:34	Says, "I freely forgive all" Rom 3:24
9	"Wages of sin is death" Rom. 6:23	"The gift of God is eternal life" Rom 6:23
10	Confirms and reveal sin Rom. 7:7	Covers and reconciles sin 2 Cor. 5:19
11	Demands obedience with no power to achieve Rom. 6:11-13; Exo. 20:7-17	Bestows and gives powers to obey Rom. 6:11-13
12	Written on stone Exo. 24:12; 31:18	Written on the heart (desires/will) 2 Cor. 3:3
13	Puts us under bondage as slaves Rom. 8:15; Gal. 2:4; 5:1	Set us free as sons of God Rom. 8:2; Gal 5:1
14	Unable to produce righteousness Gal. 3:21	Makes righteous 2 Cor. 5:21 ; Eph. 4:24
15	Gives knowledge of sin Rom. 3:20	Gives redemption from sin Titus 2:11
16	"The soul that sins shall die" Eze. 18:20	Believe and you shall live John 3:16
17	Temporary, now obsolete Gal. 3:19, 24; Heb. 8:13, 10:1	Perfect forever Heb. 8:7, 7:28, 10:12-14, 13:8
18	Can never make perfect Heb. 7:18-19	Saves to the uttermost Heb. 7:28; Gal. 3:11
19	Excludes from fellowship Eph. 2:11-12	Invites and relieves Eph. 2:13-19; Mat. 11:28
20	Death Rom. 8:2	Life Rom. 8:2

The Total Superiority of the New Covenant

ADDENDUM
"This startling, staggering message"

D. Martyn Lloyd-Jones, the great British statesmen of evangelicalism during the 1900s, wrote in *Romans, An Exposition of Chapter 6, The New Man:*[4]

"There is no better test as to whether a man is really preaching the New Testament gospel of salvation than this, that some people might misunderstand it and misinterpret it to mean that it really amounts to this, that because you are saved by grace alone it does not matter at all what you do; you can go on sinning as much as you like because it will redound all the more to the glory of grace. If my preaching and presentation of the gospel of salvation does not expose it to that misunderstanding, then it is not the gospel. Let me show you what I mean.

If a man preaches justification by works, no one would ever raise this question. If a man's preaching is, 'If you want to be Christians, and if you want to go to heaven, you must stop committing sins, you must take up good works, and if you do so regularly and constantly, and do not fail to keep on at it, you will make yourselves Christians, you will reconcile yourselves to God and you will go to heaven.'

Obviously a man who preaches in that strain would never be liable to this misunderstanding. Nobody would say to such a man, 'Shall we continue in sin, that grace may abound?', because the man's whole emphasis is just this, that if you go on sinning you are certain to be damned, and only if you stop sinning can you save yourselves. So that misunderstanding could never arise...

Nobody has ever brought this charge against the Church of Rome, but it was brought frequently against Martin Luther; indeed that was precisely what the Church of Rome said about the preaching of Martin Luther. They said, 'This man who was a priest has changed the doctrine in order to justify his own marriage and his own lust', and so on. 'This man', they said, 'is an antinomian; and that is heresy.' That is the very charge they brought against him. It was also brought George Whitfield two hundred years ago. It is the charge that formal dead Christianity – if there is such a thing – has always brought against this startling, staggering message, that God 'justifies the ungodly'...

That is my comment and it is a very important comment for preachers. I would say to all preachers: If your preaching of salvation has not been misunderstood in that way, then you had better examine your sermons again, and you had better make sure that you are really preaching the salvation that is offered in the New Testament to the ungodly, the sinner, to those who are dead in trespasses and sins, to those who are enemies of God."

The Total Superiority of the New Covenant

Find out more at
DEANBRIGGS.COM/COURSES

Get access to 10 hours of in-depth training over 58 sessions in The Total Superiority of the New Covenant *video course. Includes free 100-page Study Guide*

END NOTES

[1] Some maintain that Abraham's three visitors were really angels in the appearance of men. But Genesis 18:1 is clear: it was "the LORD" (Yahweh) who appeared to Abraham. Similarly, it is Yahweh who speaks in verses 13, 20, 26, and 33 and Abraham stands "before the LORD" in verse 22.

[2] Robert Farrar Capon, *Between Noon and Three: Romance, Law, and the Outrage of Grace* (1997); p.72, 7, Wm. B. Eerdmans Publishing; Grand Rapids, MI

[3] ibid

[4] Grand Rapids: Zondervan, 1973; pp. 9-10

Printed in Great Britain
by Amazon